MW00768399

Tennyson

A dreamer and a poet.

Mrs H

A smile and a snack for everyone.

Twigs

Ready to learn and play every day.

US Edition published in 2000
by Broadman & Holman Publishers
Nashville, Tennessee

Originally published by CWR, Waverley Abbey House, Waverley Lane, Farnham, Surrey GU9 8EP, England

Tails: King for a Day

© 1999 Karyn Henley. All rights reserved. Exclusively administered by Child Sensitive Communication, LLC
Text and characterizations by Karyn Henley
Concept development, editorial, design and production by CWR
Models created by: Debbie Casto
Photographed by: Roger Walker
Illustrations: Sheila Hardy of Advocate
Printed in Spain
ISBN 0-8054-2285-4

All rights reserved. No part of this publication may be reproduced, stored in a retrieval system, or transmitted, in any form or by any means, electronic, mechanical, photocopying, recording or otherwise, without the prior permission in writing from the publisher.

All Scripture quotations in this publication are from the Holy Bible: International Children's Bible copyright © 1983, 1988, 1991 by Word Publishing.

King for a Day

"God is King of all the earth"
Psalm 47:7

Karyn Henley

BROADMAN
&HOLMAN
PUBLISHERS

King for a Day

"Owlfred is a scientist, Mimi is an artist, Tennyson is a writer. What am I?" asked Twigs.

"You are a curious little hedgehog," said Mrs. H. "Now run along and play. I have some baking to do."

As Twigs ran along to play, he met Chester. "What's your job, Chester?" asked Twigs.

"My job is hide and seek," said Chester. "I hide nuts and then I look for where I hid them. It's a game!"

"Oh," said Twigs. "You are a game player. Owlfred is a scientist. Mimi is an artist. What am I?"

"You, my friend, are a curious little hedgehog," said Chester. "Now run along and play. I have to try to remember where I hid those nuts!"

As Twigs ran along to play, he met Owlfred.
"What are you doing?" asked Twigs.

"I'm measuring shadows," said
Owlfred. "It's an experiment!"

"You're a scientist," said Twigs.
"Mimi is an artist. Chester is a
game player. What am I?"

"You are a curious little hedgehog," said Owlfred. "Now run along and play. I must measure this shadow!"

As Twigs ran along to play, he met Tennyson. Tennyson's eyes were closed, but he was smiling. "What are you doing?" asked Twigs.

"I am writing a song," said Tennyson. "I am thinking of the words."

"You are a writer," said Twigs. "Chester is a game player. Owlfred is a scientist. What am I?"

"You are a curious little hedgehog,"
said Tennyson.

"You wonder about thunder.
You ask why about the sky.
You want to know about snow.
And that's my song, so run along."

As Twigs ran along to play, he met Mimi sitting at her easel.

"What are you doing?" asked Twigs.

"I'm getting ready to paint," said Mimi.

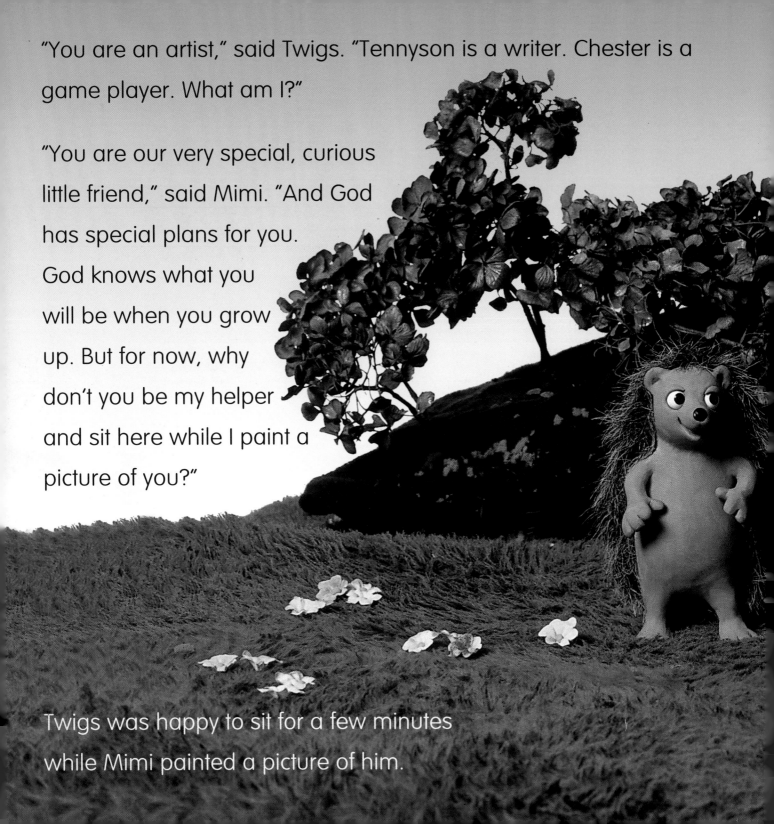

"You are an artist," said Twigs. "Tennyson is a writer. Chester is a game player. What am I?"

"You are our very special, curious little friend," said Mimi. "And God has special plans for you. God knows what you will be when you grow up. But for now, why don't you be my helper and sit here while I paint a picture of you?"

Twigs was happy to sit for a few minutes while Mimi painted a picture of him.

Then Twigs saw a book with a gold crown on the front. "What is that?" he asked.

"Those are paintings of kings," said Mimi. "Would you like to look at that book?"

"Yes!" said Twigs.

Mimi opened the book to the first picture. "The King of Beasts," she said.

"A lion!" said Twigs.

Twigs pointed to the next picture.

"Kingfisher!" said Mimi.

"A sky king!" said Twigs.

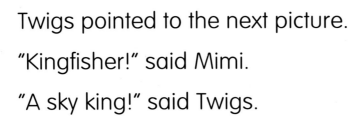

Mimi turned the page. "King Crab!" she said. "He lives in the ocean."

"A water king!" said Twigs.

"Kingcup," said Mimi.

"A plant king!" said Twigs.

"King snake!" said Mimi.

"A creepy crawly king!"
said Twigs.

Mimi closed the book. "Do you know who is the greatest king of all?" she asked.

"Who?" asked Twigs.

"God!" said Mimi. "God is the Great King, because He made the earth, the sea, and the sky. He made the plants and animals, too." Mimi began painting again.

"Yes," said Twigs. "God is the greatest King of all!"

"Do you suppose God might make me grow up to be king of hedgehogs?" asked Twigs.

"Maybe," said Mimi. "But for now, I can make you the king."

"You can?" asked Twigs. "How?"

"Like this," said Mimi. She turned her painting around so that Twigs could see it. There he was in the painting, wearing a crown!

"Hurrah!" said Twigs. "You are an artist. Owlfred is a scientist. Tennyson is a writer. Chester is a game player. And I am King Hedgehog!"

Mimi bowed. "What would you like to do now, your Majesty?" she asked.

"Hmmm," said Twigs. He thought for a moment. Then he said, "I think I would like to run along and play."

And that's just what he did!

"God is King of all the earth"

Psalm 47:7